EDDIE LEE, EDDIE LEE

A One Act Play

by Joe Sears

SAMUEL FRENCH, INC.
45 West 25th Street   NEW YORK 10010
7623 Sunset Boulevard HOLLYWOOD 90046
LONDON   TORONTO

Copyright © 1990, 1993 by Joe Sears

ALL RIGHTS RESERVED

CAUTION: Professionals and amateurs are hereby warned that EDDIE LEE, EDDIE LEE is subject to a royalty. It is fully protected under the copyright laws of the United States of America, the British Commonwealth, including Canada, and all other countries of the Copyright Union. All rights, including professional, amateur, motion picture, recitation, lecturing, public reading, radio broadcasting, television, and the rights of translation into foreign languages are strictly reserved. In its present form the play is dedicated to the reading public only.

The amateur live stage performance rights to EDDIE LEE, EDDIE LEE are controlled exclusively by Samuel French, Inc., and royalty arrangements and licenses must be secured well in advance of presentation. PLEASE NOTE that amateur royalty fees are set upon application in accordance with your producing circumstances. When applying for a royalty quotation and license please give us the number of performances intended, dates of production, your seating capacity and admission fee. Royalties are payable one week before the opening performance of the play to Samuel French, Inc., at 45 W. 25th Street, New York, NY 10010; or at 7623 Sunset Blvd., Hollywood, CA 90046, or to Samuel French (Canada), Ltd., 80 Richmond Street East, Toronto, Ontario, Canada M5C 1P1.

Royalty of the required amount must be paid whether the play is presented for charity or gain and whether or not admission is charged.

Stock royalty quoted on application to Samuel French, Inc.

For all other rights than those stipulated above, apply to Peter Franklin, c/o William Morris Agency, Inc., 1350 Ave. of the Americas, New York, NY 10019.

Particular emphasis is laid on the question of amateur or professional readings, permission and terms for which must be secured in writing from Samuel French, Inc.

Copying from this book in whole or in part is strictly forbidden by law, and the right of performance is not transferable.

Whenever the play is produced the following notice must appear on all programs, printing and advertising for the play: "Produced by special arrangement with Samuel French, Inc."

Due authorship credit must be given on all programs, printing and advertising for the play.

ISBN 0 573 69317 X   Printed in U.S.A.

No one shall commit or authorize any act or omission by which the copyright of, or the right to copyright, this play may be impaired.

No one shall make any changes in this play for the purpose of production.

Publication of this play does not imply availability for performance. Both amateurs and professionals considering a production are *strongly* advised in their own interests to apply to Samuel French, Inc., for written permission before starting rehearsals, advertising, or booking a theatre.

No part of this book may be reproduced, stored in a retrieval system, or transmitted in any form, by any means, now known or yet to be invented, including mechanical, electronic, photocopying, recording, videotaping, or otherwise, without the prior written permission of the publisher.

IMPORTANT BILLING AND CREDIT REQUIREMENTS

All producers of EDDIE LEE, EDDIE LEE *must* give credit to the Author of the Play in all programs distributed in connection with performances of the Play and in all instances in which the title of the Play appears for purposes of advertising, publicizing or otherwise exploiting the Play and/or a production. The name of the Author *must* also appear on a separate line, on which no other name appears, immediately following the title, and *must* appear in size of type not less than fifty percent the size of the title type.

CHARACTERS

EDDIE LEE, 20'S

ETTA MAY, 40'S

ALVINA, 50'S

TIME & PLACE

Present day, Helena, Montana

Eddie Lee, Eddie Lee was first workshopped at the University of Texas at Austin.

It was first produced at Northeastern State University, Tahlequah, Oklahoma.

The first professional production was at Actors Co-Op of Jackson Hole, Wyoming.

EDDIE LEE, EDDIE LEE

Present day Helena, Montana. A small and simple kitchen with an upstage left entrance to the house and an upstage right entrance to the outside. In the middle of the room at a table sits EDDIE LEE, a cowboy in his twenties. HE has passed out from drinking. HIS head is resting on the table in a very awkward and uncomfortable position. His hat is on the floor next to his chair.

ETTA MAY, a woman in her 40s, enters in a robe. It is early and somewhat dark. SHE sees Eddie Lee at the table and turns on a LIGHT. HER disgust is obvious as SHE flips the coffee maker on for one cup of coffee. SHE studies Eddie Lee then moves to the phone. SHE pushes "O" and waits.

ETTA. Morning, Jenny. I got up late. Have you opened the office?... No, I'm not sitting down, what happened? Them?... They're a church group from Laramie. Some revival band ... They did what to my walls?... There's a law in Montana against that!... Has that band checked out yet?... Jenny, you hold that little drummer there until I get dressed. And, Jenny, don't sit on that boy... You're on him now?... Jenny, don't put all your weight on him; you know what happened to that rodeo clown?... Well, if he's turning blue, let him up! Get a phone number before you do ... I'm calling Alvina's room, now ... She's there?! ... Jenny, my God! Tell Alvina to untie that boy's legs and get down here. I have a crisis of my own ... Eddie Lee again ... He's passed out *again* ... Yeah, he's drunk again ... Call me if that revival band gives you more trouble ... No, don't "revival him." Just let 'im up! *(ETTA hangs up the phone.)* My God! That woman is going on a diet or I'm facing a fat lawsuit, sure as God. Bless her heart, she means well. Not like you, Eddie Lee, who needs to wake up and smell the coffee. I know you work hard for a living and deserve your fun, but who doesn't work hard around here. And you don't see other men squandering their lives away. You have too much fun if you ask me. Just like your daddy. Only your daddy changed, Eddie Lee. He didn't want to lose his family and he changed. I'm gonna make you change if it's the last thing I do. I won't see my only son turn out like this. Tammy and the kids are waiting on you, their *daddy,* to call and here you sit like a frozen fart. Ignoring your wife to the point she tries to burn the house down. Losing your family, and hanging out with gutter-balls for friends. Well, today is your day of reckoning, Eddie Lee. And I'm leaving here with Alvina for a vacation and you can't talk me out of it. You have your own family. I've raised mine!

(ALVINA enters. A woman in her 50's. SHE is dressed in fringe and boots.)

ALVINA. Knock, knock! Etta?
ETTA. Come in, Alvina.
ALVINA. I untied that drummer.
ETTA. Good.
ALVINA. But Jenny still had him in a headlock.
ETTA. I hope she got a phone number.

ALVINA. He was struggling to write it down when I left. Will you look at what can't get up?

ETTA. He's been in that position a long time.

ALVINA. When I first met Buck, he had a permanent crease darting across his forehead from passing out like that.

ETTA. Alvina, we need to do what we talked about.

ALVINA. You mean Eddie Lee? Honey, I've already caused enough trouble with my crazy notions.

ETTA. They're desperate all right, but they work. And I'm desperate.

ALVINA. You would pick the morning we leave.

ETTA. We'll make a clean sweep of everything.

ALVINA. You're right! And it's high time he stopped whining about you going somewhere. Let him run a motel for twenty years. You're a widow, now, and like me need to get outside and get some vitamin E or you'll end up all dried like a cashew.

ETTA. I look like a pecan, now!

ALVINA. You just need a little life back in you that's all. And when we're finished with Eddie Lee this morning, he'll be a better man or a lonely one the rest of his life. You have to be brave.

ETTA. What do we do first?

ALVINA. Well, you don't want to run him out of here without a place to go. We should call Tammy and tell her to be expecting Eddie Lee.

ETTA. Tammy may not talk to me.

ALVINA. You didn't tell her to set that porch on fire. If it's anyone's fault, it's mine.

ETTA. Yea, it is. (*ETTA turns to the phone and then turns back to Alvina.*) Why don't you call her, Alvina. I think I'd start crying if one of my grandbabies answered.

ALVINA. Do you think she'll be up?

ETTA. She and the kids'll be watching the weather channel.

ALVINA. All right. But you get ready to fight with Eddie Lee.

ETTA. I'm not good at that, Alvina.

ALVINA. He's going to be mad when he wakes up.

ETTA. Why is he waking up mad?

ALVINA. 'Cause you're going to throw cold water in his face.

ETTA. I am?

ALVINA. You want to do this right, don't you? And you have to have your wits about you. Can't back off when he starts to plead. And no coffee, remember.

ETTA. What does coffee have to do with this?

ALVINA. You have to keep Eddie Lee off his guard. You have to make it hard for him to function. Put all this away. Throw these grounds away. Put away these glasses. Rinse this coffee pot. And here's the glass of water you're going to throw. He'll come up not knowing if he's on a bull or fallen in a river.

ETTA. You think we're doing the right thing?

ALVINA. He'll keep passing out like this at your table and never get his family back. You'll never get away from this motel and I'll never show you the world outside of Helena.

ETTA. Give me that glass of water.

ALVINA. Atta, girl! I'm going in here to call Tammy. I'll be listening in the next room. If I think you need help

I'll come around and knock on this door. It wouldn't hurt to have that broom ready just in case you need it.

ETTA. I don't think I could hit Eddie Lee.

ALVINA. He would never hit you so use that against him. Here. The broom's right here if you need it.

ETTA. I don't know about this, Alvina.

ALVINA. Ooh, give me that water.

(ALVINA throws the glass of water on Eddie Lee. SHE hands the glass to ETTA and runs out up left. ETTA sets the glass on the table and runs for the broom. EDDIE LEE stirs awake rather quickly and sits straight up as HE gives a rebel yell. HE stares into space and drops his lower jaw as HE exhales with a loud moan. HE's dazed and yells again.)

EDDIE LEE. Son-of-a-bitch!! *(HE sticks his tongue out and wrinkles his face.)* Damn. Somebody shit in my mouth.

(HE sees the glass of water and starts to reach for it. ETTA is quicker and grabs the glass first.)

ETTA. You don't get another thing from me.

(HE motions for her to hand him the water.)

ETTA. Not until we have discussed your antics.

(HE weakly motions for the water.)

ETTA. Something we should have done a long time ago.

(HE moans.)

ETTA. Not until you've heard me out, Eddie Lee. You don't live here, you know!

(HE tries to get out of the seat but can't. HE sighs.)

ETTA. Staying out all hours pushing over cows in their sleep. And whatever else it is you do with your good-for-nothing friend, Charlie. Passing out like some hobo every other night. What's wrong with you, Eddie Lee? You are no longer welcome under this roof. You can't pass out here anymore. You can't even visit, do you hear me?
EDDIE LEE. Mama, you're making me sick.
ETTA. You think it makes me feel good to see you waste your life and family away? I won't watch it. Not anymore, Eddie Lee.
EDDIE LEE. I'm not up yet, Mama. Don't start.
ETTA. Tammy started it. I'm going to finish it.
EDDIE LEE. I need some coffee.
ETTA. Forget it.
EDDIE LEE. I'll take some water.
ETTA. Not anymore, Eddie Lee. Nothing.
EDDIE LEE. Can't you say "Good morning, son?"
ETTA. Good morning, Eddie Lee. Where did you go last night? Shoot out any lights?
EDDIE LEE. Mama, I'm gonna be real sick if you don't give me that glass of water.

ETTA. You throw up, you'll clean it up. (*SHE hits him with a broom.*)

EDDIE LEE. I can't get up.

ETTA. You're like some buffalo stuck in the mud—not having sense enough to know which leg to pull out first.

EDDIE LEE. Mama, just make me some coffee and shut up.

ETTA. My guests don't tell me to shut up. (*SHE hits him with broom.*)

EDDIE LEE. Alvina's got you smoking pot?

ETTA. Alvina does not smoke pot.

EDDIE LEE. She chews loco weed. Why wouldn't she smoke it?

ETTA. You leave Alvina out of this.

EDDIE LEE. Where's she coming from this time, Libya?

ETTA. I want to know where you were last night when you should have been with your family. (*SHE hits him with broom.*)

EDDIE LEE. I don't have a family, remember?

ETTA. You let that great little wife you have slip through your fingers.

EDDIE LEE. My wife set fire to the house!

ETTA. She set fire to the front porch.

EDDIE LEE. My kids were there. They could have been hurt.

ETTA. She had them with her in the yard. Don't you think those poor little babies are ruined after watching their mama set fire to the house? (*SHE hits him again.*)

EDDIE LEE. Hell, you act like it's my fault she set fire to the house. Please, please, please get me a glass of water.

ETTA. Get it yourself. Better get used to fixing your own coffee and waiting on Eddie Lee. Nobody around here is gonna do it.

(EDDIE LEE manages to get up and make it to the sink where HE hugs the cabinet, ready to vomit. HE turns on the water and drinks out of his hand.)

ETTA. I'm tired of people telling me about you being drunk and the things you do. I'm a respectable woman in this town with a good business.

EDDIE LEE. I'm just having fun.

ETTA. I think you have too much fun if you wanna to ask somebody.

(EDDIE LEE reaches for the cabinet and ETTA swats him with broom.)

ETTA. Get your own glass.

EDDIE LEE. If I move I'm gonna be sick.

ETTA. Eddie Lee, Eddie Lee.

EDDIE LEE. Mama, please stop. (*HE reaches for the coffee container and uses it as a glass.*)

ETTA. Maybe you'll see how bad it is to let your family go. I can't take seeing you like this, coming in from God-knows-where with that worthless Charlie. Like two old alley cats sharing a dumpster. (*SHE swats him with broom.*)

EDDIE LEE. What the hell is wrong with you this morning?

ETTA. Don't you think you go out too much, Eddie Lee?

EDDIE LEE, EDDIE LEE

EDDIE LEE. Can't you ask me something else?

ETTA. You don't live here anymore. You're a guest and I can ask my guests anything I like.

EDDIE LEE. A guest in my own mama's house.

ETTA. Sad, isn't it?

EDDIE LEE. If Daddy were here, he'd see things different.

ETTA. He's not here, though, is he?

EDDIE LEE. He'd speak up for me. Nobody sets fire to their house without being crazy. You want me to go back and live with a crazy woman? Charlie said I could get custody of the kids based on the fire alone.

ETTA. What does Charlie know about anything? And wouldn't you make a fine daddy, raising two kids by yourself? You'd have them one afternoon before they'd be taken away. You're gonna have to grow up. You are headed down some one-way streets, baby.

EDDIE LEE. How do you make this coffee?!

ETTA. Figure it out.

EDDIE LEE. Hell, Mama.

ETTA. Hell, what?

EDDIE LEE. What's wrong with you? Have you been watching those talk shows again?

ETTA. I should put you on Donahue's show. You can talk about men who never grow up.

EDDIE LEE. I can talk about men having fun.

ETTA. Yeah, you could tell the audience how you pushed over that cow in it's sleep.

EDDIE LEE. You need help in the motel, is that it?

ETTA. When have you ever helped me in the motel?

EDDIE LEE. Are you missing Daddy?

ETTA. He never helped either. He never did anything but watch that TV tube.

EDDIE LEE. You missed him when he died.

ETTA. Of course I did. I had to change the channels myself.

EDDIE LEE. And you miss him now.

ETTA. Like I miss Monday night football. Eddie Lee, Eddie Lee, don't make me say these things. You know I loved your father!

EDDIE LEE. I never heard you complain about Daddy.

ETTA. It's none of your business what I complain about.

EDDIE LEE. Why didn't you make him get up and go somewhere?

ETTA. Spent too much time getting him to stay home. Your daddy was kinda wild, Eddie Lee.

EDDIE LEE. My daddy? He was a good bull-rider and they have fun, that's all.

ETTA. He was too wild, Eddie Lee. We had to leave Oklahoma! We had to leave a state.

EDDIE LEE. Why?

ETTA. Some things happened back in Tulsa that I won't go into.

EDDIE LEE. Why not?

ETTA. Cause it's none of your business. We moved back here and took over Daddy's motel and you were born and now I'm facing Tulsa in the face!

EDDIE LEE. What happened? Is there something I should know about?

ETTA. No. We should never have brought it up.

EDDIE LEE. Am I going to die of cancer or something?

ETTA. No!

EDDIE LEE. You need to stop watching those talk shows.

ETTA. I don't know how to explain it. One day you'll wake up and ask yourself, "What in the heck have I done with my life?" If you're not happy with the answer, there's nothing you can do except keep going and hope that what you're headed for is worth waiting on. Sometimes that can be something as simple as love. Sometimes it's the very thing that holds you back and yet without love you never had a chance at life to begin with. Good or bad, you latch on to love. Let it be the most important thing in your life. Even if you end up with something as empty as this motel I live in.

EDDIE LEE. There you go, sounding like a talk show.

ETTA. Eddie Lee, Eddie Lee, honey, I'm speaking to you from my heart.

EDDIE LEE. Still sounds like Donahue to me.

ETTA. I don't listen to talk shows anymore. That was my lost period.

EDDIE LEE. Donahue had you ready to change your name.

ETTA. I didn't, did I?

EDDIE LEE. You tried to. And after that you thought you had a twin somewhere in the world.

ETTA. I was on medication.

EDDIE LEE. Then you thought old Sparky was an alien space pet.

ETTA. He has six thumbs.

EDDIE LEE. It hurts me to see my Mama go crazy.

ETTA. I'm crazy because we finally have this out? You would blame a deer tick if you thought you could get by with it.

EDDIE LEE. You've been watching too many talk shows!

ETTA. And you've been masturbating on my sheets.

EDDIE LEE. What the hell?

ETTA. A fine looking man like you having to do something like that when you have a pretty wife to take care of those needs.

EDDIE LEE. Mama!

ETTA. A grown man! Next thing you know you and Charlie will start doing it together.

EDDIE LEE. That's enough!

ETTA. You bet it is. You're not ruining anymore of my sheets.

EDDIE LEE. All this bitching because I went to a rodeo last weekend.

ETTA. Every weekend.

EDDIE LEE. I try to win money.

ETTA. What money? You spend more time eating dirt than you do on the back of one of them buckin' horses.

EDDIE LEE. You didn't have to say that.

ETTA. Eddie Lee, Eddie Lee. This dream you're holding on to is bigger and meaner than that beast you try to ride.

EDDIE LEE. You just said you have to hold on to something meaningful in life.

ETTA. Your wife and kids will never buck you off, Eddie Lee.

EDDIE LEE. You don't want me to have any fun?

ETTA. Don't seek it out. If you're living the right life and doing what you're supposed to be doing, fun will come to you.

EDDIE LEE. Donahue again.

ETTA. Fun does not put food on the table. What did you do with it, Eddie Lee?

EDDIE LEE. With what?

ETTA. Your paycheck. You went off to that rodeo with your paycheck. You left babies and a wife at home without proper groceries. Virginia and Pat had to bring their daughter food. What did you do with it?

EDDIE LEE. I left it in the motel room and the maid got it.

ETTA. You expect me to believe that? No wonder Tammy set fire to the house.

EDDIE LEE. Whose side are you on, Mama?

ETTA. You need to pick up that phone and call your family, young man.

EDDIE LEE. I got things to do. I have to repair that porch.

ETTA. You need to repair your life!

EDDIE LEE. I like my life!

ETTA. Right now you do but what about tomorrow when you wake up on planet earth?

EDDIE LEE. I can't take any more of this without coffee. My friends think I'm a pretty good ol' boy.

ETTA. Charlie tell you that?

EDDIE LEE. There's nothing wrong with Charlie.

ETTA. He's almost forty years old and he's facing the middle alone. His good times are only as good as the company he keeps. He's a scared man and I don't ever want you to be like that. You can change now, while you're still young.

EDDIE LEE. Charlie ain't so bad. Alvina's been with him. She put out for him.

ETTA. Eddie Lee, you should never say that about Alvina. *(SHE hits him with broom.)*

EDDIE LEE. I didn't mean that.

ETTA. She's one of the few friends you have that amounts to anything. I never told you this, you remember that fire truck your daddy got you for Christmas? You used to say it was your favorite Christmas present.

EDDIE LEE. I remember.

ETTA. Alvina gave you that fire truck.

EDDIE LEE. Daddy gave me that fire truck.

ETTA. We couldn't even pay the light bill let alone get you a nice present. Alvina and Buck arrived on Christmas eve with that truck. She didn't know we were in bad shape. She insisted your daddy make that present from him.

EDDIE LEE. You didn't have to tell me that.

ALVINA. *(Enters UR.)* Knock, knock. Never mind. I'm already in the door.

ETTA. Morning, Alvina.

(EDDIE LEE is now at the sink rubbing water over his head and face. ALVINA moves to his side and gets the towel that EDDIE is reaching for. SHE dabs the cloth on his head and begins cleaning her blouse.)

ALVINA. How are you today, rascal? Excuse me but I need a little dab of water. This fringe picks up every little piece of dirt. I'm not saying Jenny hasn't cleaned my room very well. Last night I danced with a rough one. There was a time I liked smelling crude oil on a man.

ETTA. I'd offer you some coffee, but ...

ALVINA. But Eddie Lee hasn't figured out how to make it yet.

EDDIE LEE. You want some coffee, you make it.

ALVINA. You're not roping me into this little war.

EDDIE LEE. You're probably the one who talked her into this rampage.

ETTA. Eddie Lee, you watch yourself.

ALVINA. I'll admit it, "Stink-pot."

EDDIE LEE. And don't call me "Stink-pot." You do that in front of my friends.

ALVINA. Excuse me, but who am I? I'm the one who helped change your shitty little pants.

EDDIE LEE. You don't have to call me that in front of people.

ALVINA. Just make sure you never let anyone else call you my pet name. That's reserved for me only. That's what's special about knowing me.

EDDIE LEE. There's nothing special about you.

ALVINA. Well, your mama has stirred something up. Give me an update, Etta.

ETTA. I've told Eddie Lee he's no longer welcome in my house.

ALVINA. Good for you.

EDDIE LEE. See, I was right, you're in on this.

ALVINA. What else?

ETTA. I told him he should go back to his wife.

ALVINA. Did you tell him how worthless he is?

ETTA. I didn't say no such thing, Alvina.

ALVINA. Did you tell him how bad it is to go through life alone?

EDDIE LEE. I'll get by.

ALVINA. Did you tell him you're going with me?

EDDIE LEE. No. She hasn't!

ETTA. Let me get you some coffee, Alvina.

ALVINA. No, you don't. You don't go near that coffee maker.

EDDIE LEE. Let her make some coffee. Hell, the two of you are gonna damn sure kill me.

ALVINA. Then your mama won't have to worry about you ever again, will she?

EDDIE LEE. Why don't you go back to your room, Alvina?

ETTA. I say who's welcome and who isn't.

ALVINA. We both know I'm welcome here so why don't you go upstairs and pack your paper bag?

EDDIE LEE. Both of you ganging up on me.

ALVINA. Etta, if he's not going to pack, you need to. We still have to go to K-Mart and pick out your new outfits.

EDDIE LEE. Where's she going? Where are you going?

ETTA. To K-Mart to pick out new outfits.

ALVINA. You know me. I go everywhere. I see people and places and have a good time. Hell, I know every crevice of Montana.

EDDIE LEE. My mama plays bingo. She don't go to bars.

ETTA. Eddie Lee!

ALVINA. You have never seen me behave any way but like a lady. Now you apologize to me.

EDDIE LEE. I'm sorry.

ALVINA. Your mama is not going in some old bar.
ETTA. I might.
ALVINA. I'm going to Wyoming on business. I want your mama to go with me and she wants to go.
ETTA. Eddie Lee said you went out with Charlie.
ALVINA. I did?
ETTA. Charlie told the boys he had his way with you.
EDDIE LEE. Mama, you didn't have to tell her that.
ETTA. I won't have my son out with a man like that.
ALVINA. Etta, why don't you go get dressed. The blue light special only comes on twice a day. I want to talk to "Stink-pot."
ETTA. All right. Eddie Lee, you listen to Alvina.
EDDIE LEE. I don't live here, remember? I don't have to do a goddamn thing.

(ETTA exits. EDDIE LEE turns and steps on his hat. HE tries to reshape it.)

EDDIE LEE. I have to go, Alvina. I'm gonna get some coffee. (*HE pulls out his wallet.*) Son-of-a-bitch. Alvina, could you loan me a dollar?
ALVINA. Sit down, Eddie Lee. I'll make you the best cup of coffee in the world.
EDDIE LEE. I know that's right. About time somebody around here loved me.

(ALVINA moves to the refrigerator for the coffee can and starts making coffee. When SHE fills the coffee container with water, SHE eyes the level carefully and pours out a small amount, the perfect amount, for the best cup of coffee in the world.)

ALVINA. The problem is too many women love you, Eddie Lee. And I know you can't help being pretty. Your daddy was a pretty man. He looked good coming out of chute number three, all spurs and poise and then right into the dirt he'd go. But a fine looking man coming out of the chutes. I knew him before your mama did. Your mama never went to the rodeo until she started dating your daddy. I knew your mama and her folks here at the motel. They put me up in the same cottage I'm in now. I always stay in the same cottage, it's traditional.

EDDIE LEE. I know all this.

ALVINA. Your mother was so fascinated with me. She was so young and beautiful and full of wonder. I helped her put on proper make-up and to this day your mama wears only the right amount. (*ALVINA looks at the progress of the coffee.*) Did your mama ever tell you how she met your daddy?

EDDIE LEE. Many times, Alvina.

ALVINA. How he drove his pickup off Spirit Bluff and broke his collar bone. And your mama was the prettiest candy striper. I guess your daddy didn't have any choice about falling in love. He couldn't go back to rodeo with that collar bone the way it was. I didn't like your daddy at first but then he changed and I grew real fond of him.

EDDIE LEE. Daddy said he had lots of girl friends back then.

ALVINA. He did. But your mama roped and tied him in five seconds. It's good to have women after you. Keeps them healthy and fit.

EDDIE LEE. They ain't nothing but a lot of trouble.

ALVINA. Like I said, too many women love you. And of all the women who love you, me included, is your wife, Tammy. Now there's an important love to have with you. It's the very best kind of love because you can see just behind Tammy's eyes when she's looking at you. That look is pure unadulterated love. Other men see that love first. Women never recognize it but men do because it's their nature to look for any signs of weakness. They want to know if there is true happiness behind those eyes, and what those men see behind Tammy's eyes is true love.

EDDIE LEE. I love her, too.

ALVINA. I know that. Tammy knows that. That's why she set fire to the house. (*ALVINA looks st the progress of the coffee.*) And there's the woman who is your mother. Her love is the strongest and most protective. It's our nature to love and trust mama. Her love holds the clan together. It's that kind of love that holds nations together. That coffee should be ready.

EDDIE LEE. I'll take it black.

ALVINA. I knew there was a man inside you. (*SHE hands him a cup of coffee.*)

EDDIE LEE. That's good coffee, Alvina. About the best I've ever had.

ALVINA. I wish I had a nickle for every time I've heard that. You know, a man's best moments are right after a hangover. He's so glad to be back in the world again.

EDDIE LEE. I think I better stop drinking so much. And pushing over cows in their sleep.

ALVINA. No more throwing beer bottles at signs along the road.

EDDIE LEE. I only did that once.

ALVINA. Yes, but you hit the sheriff.

EDDIE LEE. I didn't see 'im.

ALVINA. You were drunk.

EDDIE LEE. I don't do this all the time.

ALVINA. Enough you have a reputation. It's breaking your mother's heart and you need to stop.

EDDIE LEE. Straighten up and fly right as Grandma use to say.

ALVINA. You'll have to, Eddie Lee, or someday you'll look in the mirror and see Charlie looking back.

EDDIE LEE. Don't start on Charlie. Mama's already gone off on that.

ALVINA. Your mama don't know Charlie like we do. I've known Charlies all my life. I've watched many party their lives away. When they get older they erect these big beer guts that spill over their belts like some Hoover Dam. They sit around the bar moaning and groaning like unmilked cows.

(EDDIE LEE smiles and nods in recognition. EDDIE LEE laughs. ALVINA takes his cup and gets him another cup of coffee.)

ALVINA. But the saddest part is when they lose everything that matters in their life. They don't have families anymore. So they sit around hugging beers the rest of their lives. (*ALVINA looks at EDDIE LEE who is off in thought.*)

EDDIE LEE. What?

ALVINA. So Charlie said he had his way with me, huh?

EDDIE LEE. I never believed it.

ALVINA. Nor did anyone else he was dumb enough to tell. One night in Cheyenne, he gave me a ride back to my hotel. That's all there is to Alvina and Charlie.

EDDIE LEE. I should punch his lights out.

ALVINA. You leave Charlie alone. He wants to be around winners. That's why he hangs onto you so much. You're a winner and he knows it.

EDDIE LEE. I'm not a winner. I can't stay on a buckin' horse.

ALVINA. Neither could your daddy. You're the winner, you, the person Eddie Lee. You're the one who has good looks and confidence. You're funny. People like you. Look at Jesse Hollins. Now there's a man with confidence and poise. And, what a gentleman!

EDDIE LEE. Yeah, I know 'im.

ALVINA. You're just like him. Well, he's matured now but there was a time he rode the wildest things in and out of the arena. He grew up one day. I came through here and saw him at the supermarket helping his wife shop for groceries. I didn't think much about it until I spotted him at the Moose Lodge dinner up in Bozeman. Hell, that's the wildest party in Montana. There he was having a ball with his wife and friends. He wasn't drunk, turning over tables or starting fights. People admired him for who he really was. I was so impressed I even walked over and wanted to be his friend. That's charisma and some day your charisma will come out and when you walk through the door with that pretty and loving Tammy on your arm, all eyes will rise to greet you. And this fine lady will be there to do the cotton-eyed Joe with the best damn man in the place. And I won't call you "Stink-pot" either. I'll call you my Eddie

Lee, the man I always knew he was. (*ALVINA ruffles his hair and kisses him.*)

EDDIE LEE. But Tammy set fire to the house!

ALVINA. So. Your mama did it first, years ago.

EDDIE LEE. My mama set fire to the house? When?!

ALVINA. Back in Tulsa. She hasn't told you that?

EDDIE LEE. No!

ALVINA. Oh, dear.

EDDIE LEE. Mama set fire to the house?

ALVINA. She set fire to the porch, there's a difference.

EDDIE LEE. That's where Tammy got the idea!! From my own mama!

ALVINA. Well, it was sort of my idea. We had it all planned out. There was never any real danger. Your mama set that fire knowing your daddy was coming home for dinner on time.

EDDIE LEE. Well, I didn't come home on time!

ALVINA. Well, Tammy didn't have good timing. Nobody told Tammy to set that fire. She overheard your mama and me talking about Tulsa and your daddy's younger years.

EDDIE LEE. What did Daddy do?

ALVINA. Well, he was plenty mad. He did quit that playing poker 'till all hours and your mama had groceries after that. The best thing that happened was your mama stayed with him and then you were born.

EDDIE LEE. That's no way to settle things. Settin' fire to the house.

ALVINA. Honey, people do strange things when they're fighting for survival.

EDDIE LEE. All Tammy wants to do is watch the weather channel.

ALVINA. You should do more together.

EDDIE LEE. Watches it like she's taking a test. She's got the kids doing it!

ALVINA. She needs you, Eddie Lee. She's reaching out for help.

EDDIE LEE. She needs help all right. I woke up one morning tied up in extension cords, Alvina!

ALVINA. You slapped her the night before!

EDDIE LEE. I didn't even remember it.

ALVINA. You were drunk.

EDDIE LEE. She could have killed me with those extension cords.

ALVINA. She didn't hurt you.

EDDIE LEE. She was going to plug me in, Alvina. I had never hit her before. She could have forgiven me.

ALVINA. And forgive you the next time and the time after that until she's black and blue with all her brothers after your butt.

EDDIE LEE. I ain't that kind of man.

ALVINA. A real *man* would never hit a woman the first time.

EDDIE LEE. Bullshit!

ALVINA. Tammy needs company, Eddie Lee. That's why she bought out that pet store when she got all those gerbils.

EDDIE LEE. She didn't have to put one in my lunchbox. I nearly fell off that scaffolding.

ALVINA. Why don't you do more things together.

EDDIE LEE. I watch the weather channel with her. And when I'm tired of that I can go out knowing it's raining down in Shreveport.

ALVINA. Eddie Lee, Eddie Lee.

EDDIE LEE. And if someone was to ask me what the pollen index is, I'll know that too!

ALVINA. She wants to travel life's highway with you.

EDDIE LEE. She'll know where the roads are slick.

ALVINA. Take her to the rodeo's with you.

EDDIE LEE. She stayed in the motel and watched the weather channel.

ALVINA. Maybe Tammy set fire to the house to get your attention. It worked for your mama.

EDDIE LEE. Was my daddy that bad?

ALVINA. When your daddy was young he had some wild oats to seed. He was a good man you know that. He just fell out of life after his porch was set on fire. He went overboard to keep your mama. He left Tulsa and that wild life and brought your mama back here where she belonged. He changed his life to keep her and to your daddy that meant no compromises. He completely changed like night and day and some of that daylight never came back. He was like some mustang that got caught and tamed that never should have been caught in the first place. He chose to keep his family. To do that, he had to be tamed. *(Pause.)* And that's when we became good friends. He liked hearing about all the places Buck and I had been to. You remember Buck?

EDDIE LEE. Yeah.

ALVINA. I know you were little, but you remember him. Buck was a fun man to be with. Everyone knew him and if something happened in Jackson Hole, he was consulted. A wild man, though, without me on his arm. I tamed him and he showed me the world. We could walk into a party and upstage the governor, he was so popular. Did it once, too, at Old Faithful Lodge. God, we were a pair. Everyone respected **Buck and** that's why they respect me today. I am Buck and he was me and that's what love and fun is all about. You'll see soon enough. You've got that good man hiding right there behind your shirt. You'll let it out when the time comes. Now, you think about picking up that phone **and calling** Tammy so she can be with that good man of hers.

EDDIE LEE. I said **some bad** things to her over that porch.

ALVINA. She's not stupid. She knows you don't set fire to the house and not get people mad.

ETTA. *(Enters.)* I see you broke down and made some coffee, Eddie Lee. I don't believe it.

ALVINA. And it's good. Here, let me fix you a cup of the best coffee in the world.

ETTA. I'm glad somebody's in a good mood. Did you tell him we're going to Crow Fair?

EDDIE LEE. Crow Fair? My mama ain't going to no Indian Reservation.

ALVINA. A retailer in Kansas City pays me a lot of money to pick out nice, fine jewelry at Crow Fair. Your mama wants to see how much fun it is to spend other people's money.

ETTA. Eddie Lee, this coffee is wonderful. I can't believe you made this.

EDDIE LEE. I didn't. Alvina made it.

ALVINA. I never could tell this boy "no."

(EDDIE LEE is off in thought.)

ETTA. What did you two talk about?
ALVINA. Things.

ETTA. What things?

ALVINA. Good things.

ETTA. Like what?

ALVINA. About Tammy, and how she set fire to the house.

ETTA. The porch.

ALVINA. Why she set fire to the porch. And just other things.

ETTA. What other things? *(ETTA looks at Eddie Lee who is still off in thought.)* Eddie Lee?

EDDIE LEE. What?

ETTA. What other things did you and Alvina talk about?

EDDIE LEE. We ... *(EDDIE LEE looks at Alvina.)* We talked about Buck and Daddy. *(HE smiles.)* Alvina, can I have another cup of that best coffee in the world?

ALVINA. You sure can and for you I'll even make a fresh pot. *(ALVINA begins to repeat the same process as before only quicker.)*

EDDIE LEE. *(Walks over to Etta and kisses her on the head.)* Have fun at Crow Fair. Don't let her trade you off for a pair of earrings.

ETTA. I'll be fine.

EDDIE LEE. I know.

(HE walks to the phone and starts to dial. ETTA watches him as does ALVINA who is still making coffee.)

EDDIE LEE. Hello, Charlie? Sorry to wake you up, man, but I'm not going to the rodeo this weekend ... changed my mind. I'm going to get Tammy and the kids. I'm bringing them home.

(HE hangs up. The TWO WOMEN glance at each other. EDDIE LEE is dialing again. ALVINA makes nervous small talk.)

ALVINA. You know, Etta, I think we need to take in the Custer Battlefield while we're there in Crow Fair.
ETTA. I've seen Custer's Battlefield.
ALVINA. We could go gamble in Billings.
ETTA. I've done that, too.
ALVINA. We could stay here and watch the weather channel.

(The WOMEN are silent now as THEY wait for the phone to answer on the other end of Eddie Lee's call.)

EDDIE LEE. Hello, Tammy?... I'm sorry I hadn't called sooner. I've been busy with a couple of hellcats ... Oh, nothing, just saying goodbye to a couple of stray cats. How are the kids?... Yeah, I miss them, too!... No, honey, don't put 'em on, you're the one I want to talk to ... I know ... I know ...

(ETTA has covered her tears of joy. ALVINA gets her up.)

ALVINA. Come on, let's get out to K-Mart. What he doesn't know is after we load ourselves up with jewelry, we're going back to Billings and have dinner with Red Childers.
ETTA. Red Childers? Is he still around?
ALVINA. Still around.

EDDIE LEE. I love you, too, Tammy ... That's all over, honey.

ALVINA. Leave that coffee on. That man deserves the whole pot.

(THEY smile at Eddie Lee as THEY leave. EDDIE LEE is still talking to Tammy when the LIGHTS fade.)

EDDIE LEE. I'm not doing that anymore. And we're not staying home to watch weather. Hell, we'll go where it is.

END OF PLAY

COSTUME

<u>Eddie Lee</u>
Cowboy shirt and white T-shirt
Wrangler jeans with belt
Cowboy boots
Cowboy hat

<u>Etta</u>
Night gown
House coat
Slippers
Pantsuit or dress ensemble with blouse
Shoes
Purse

<u>Alvina</u>
Western skirt or jeans
Western fancy fringe blouse
Boots
Indian jewelry
Purse

PROPERTY

<u>Full</u> <u>Kitchen</u> <u>set</u> <u>or</u> <u>Fragmentary</u>
Kitchen Table and 2 chairs
Ice Box
Stove
Running water in a sink—cabinet unit
Cupboards above cabinets
Wall telephone
Broom
Drinking glass (unbreakable)
Dishes in a drainer
Coffee maker (drip)
2 coffee cups

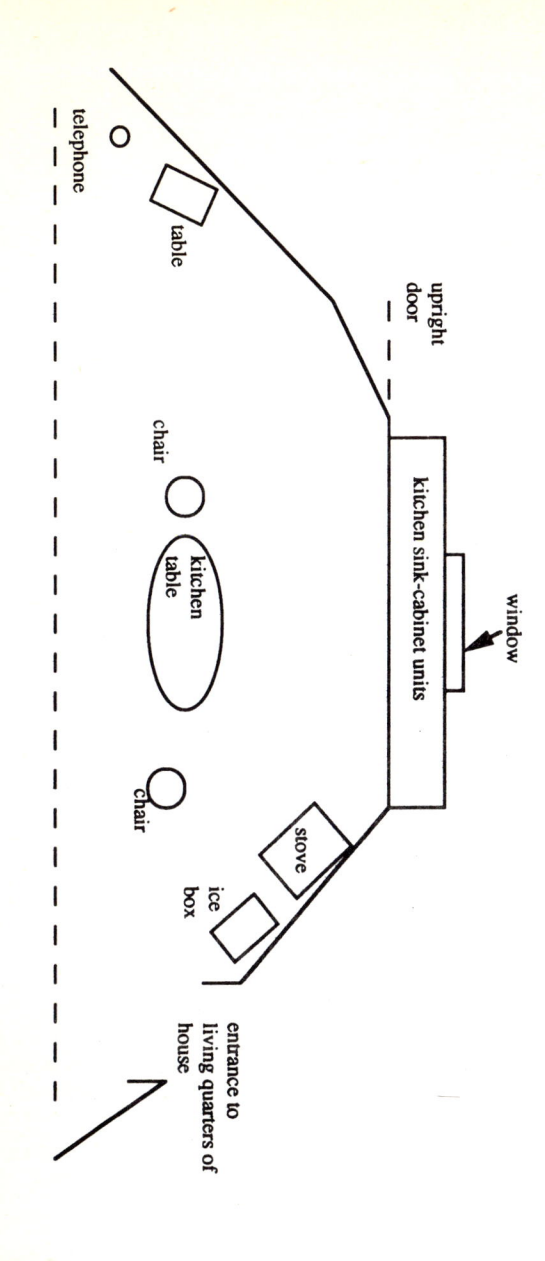

EDDIE LEE, EDDIE LEE
GROUND PLAN

Other Publications For Your Interest

SIS BOOM BAA. Comedy. Sybil Rosen. 2m., 4f. Int. Football widows of America: This Is Your Life! Pam, Cheryl, Linda and Mary are best friends. They do everything together—because their husbands spend most of their time watching football on TV. Says Pam: "Compulsive football-watching is a male-reaction formation to the stress of being civilized. It's more bonding than Crazy Glue." Mary, the new-comer to the group has recently married Joey, and his obsession is really getting to her. While the women cook New Year's Day dinner in Cheryl's kitchen they coach Mary on technique—on how to get Joey's attention away from the game. We finally meet Joey when he comes into the kitchen for something to eat; and Mary tries what she has learned on him, to no avail—so she tackles him! (#21681)

FREEZE TAG. Comedy. Jacquelyn Reingold. 2f Ext. When Andrea tries to buy a newspaper in NYC's East Village, she is thrust onto an emotional journey she will never forget. Aldrich, the newsstand vendor, seems to know the most intimate secrets of Andrea's life, from childhood up to the present moment, including who her boyfriend is sleeping with and why. In this funny and touching play, two women are forced to confront who they are, who they once were, and what it means to be a friend. "Gripping and hilarious."—N.Y. Times. "Really terrific . . . one of the most impressive [playwriting] debuts of the season."—N.Y. Press. "An extraordinary play . . . an unforgettable experience."—Back Stage. (#8678)

LOOKIN' FOR A BETTER BERRY BUSH. Comic Drama. Jean Lenox Toddie (author of *Tell Me Another Story Sing Me a Song, A Scent of Honeysuckle* and *A Bag of Green Apples*). 2f. Ext. (simply suggested). Emma and Addie confront each other on the sidewalk of a city neighborhood. Emma is a proper woman who worked in a diner for forty years and "served more cups of coffee than you can count if you live to be a hundred." Addie, a street woman whose papa "set us t' wanderin' jes' a-lookin' fer a better berry bush," rummages in trash cans and sleeps in a cardboard box. This is the humorous and touching tale of two women, alienated from each other by vastly different life experience, who clash on a city street, only to find themselves sitting down together on a stoop in front of a brownstone, and tentatively reaching out for mutual understanding. (#14927)

Penguin Blues

by Ethan Phillips

Comic Drama. 1m., 1f. Int. This beautiful short play by actor Ethan Phillips of TV's "Benson" wowed them at Philadelphia Festival Theatre for New Plays. The critics were unanimous in their praise. We are in a room in an alcoholism rehabilitation center. The characters are Gordon, a manic alcoholic who knows the score, and Angelica, a nun who denies that she is an alcoholic. In the moving climax, Angelica finally recognizes why she is there; and in so doing, takes the painful first step towards sobriety. "One of the loveliest moments of emotional revelation I've seen in the theatre."—News of Delaware County.

(#18934)

Portfolio

by Tom Donaghy

Comedy. 1m., 1f., plus 1 offstage voice. Int. This amusing satire of advertising was produced to great audience mirth and critical approval at NYC's famed comedy theatre, Manhattan Punchline. We are on a photo shoot for a print ad campaign. The photographer, who is present only by voice, has had the brilliant idea to deck his model with live pigeons. He's hired a "pigeon man" to bring in a truckload of them. He becomes most annoyed, though, when the pigeons (which are mimed, by the way), won't take direction as easily as the model, much to the distress of the hapless pigeon man. Meanwhile, the model remains unflappable. In her business, she's used to anything and everything! (#18952)

Haiku

by Katherine Snodgrass

Drama. 3f., Int. This sublimely beautiful short play won the prestigious Heidemann Award given by the Actors Theatre of Louisville, perhaps the most important one-act play award in the United States. The story concerns a woman who lives with her retarded daughter, who has miraculously at brief intervals been "normal." In fact, the daughter, Louise, is sometimes super-normal, speaking in beautiful haiku poetry, which her mother has recorded and has had published under the mother's name. Then an older daughter, Billie, comes for a visit. Billie only knows her sister as hopelessly retarded, and refuses to believe that her mother's poetry has actually been composed by her sister. (#10650)

INCIDENT AT SAN BAJO
Drama
by Brad Korbesmeyer

3m., 4f. Bare Stage. The residents of a trailer camp at San Bajo have quite a story to tell, about a stranger who visited each one in turn, selling a mysterious elixir which he claimed would make them "live longer." Most of the residents of San Bajo did not buy the elixir of course—and they are now dead, the water supply having been poisoned by the mysterious stranger. Only seven are left to tell the tale—the seven who drank the elixir which, it turned out, was an antidote! Each tells his story in a series of interlocking monologues given to an unseen interviewer. The effect is somewhat like a "60 Minutes" segment, with an imaginary Morley Safer. This most unusual new play was the 1988 winner of Actors Theatre of Louisville's Heidemann Award, perhaps the most prestigious one-act play award in the United States. (#11654)

BAIT AND SWITCH
Comedy
by Richard Dresser

3m., 2f. Int. Doug and Gary own and run a restaurant on the boardwalk which is fast going under, largely due to a recent influx of stinging jellyfish which has kept customers away from the beach, but also due to the fact that the two brothers are less than adept businessmen—particularly Gary, who isn't even aware that his brother is skimming profits. Their only hope is Kenny, a slick wiseguy with possible Mob connections. Kenny meets with Gary and Doug, sizes up the situation immediately, and eventually does take over the restaurant, forcing the two brothers out and, possibly, ending up with Gary's wife Lucy as part of the deal. Another incisive comic look at the American entrepreneurial mentality from the author of *The Downside, Better Days* and *Alone at the Beach*. (#3948)